Double
Trouble
Press

ABCs of Empowering your Dyslexic Child: Nurturing Strength Through Faith

Written By: Erika McCallister

Always remember, you are amazing just the way you are.

Psalm 139:14 - "I am fearfully and wonderfully made; your works are wonderful, I know that full well."

Believe in yourself, you have incredible potential.

Philippians 4:13 - "I can do all things through him who gives me strength."

Challenges make you stronger, and you can conquer them.

Romans 8:37 - "Know, in all these things we are more than conquerors through him who loved us."

Dyslexia is just one part of you, and it does not define who you are.

Psalm 139:13 - "For you created my inner most being; you knitted me together in my mother's womb."

Every effort you make is a step towards success.

Colossians 3:23 - "Whatever you do, work at it with all your heart, as working for the Lord, not for others."

Focus on your strengths, they are unique and valuable.

1 Peter 4:10 - "You should use whatever gift you have received to serve others, as faithful stewards of God's grace."

Growth and progress are more important than perfection.

G

2 Corinthians 12:9 - "'My grace is sufficient for you, for my power is made perfect in weakness.'"

Hold your head high, you are a special and creative individual.

1 Peter 2:9 - "But you are a chosen people, a royal priesthood, a holy nation, that you may declare the praises of him who called you out of darkness into his wonderful light."

It's okay to ask for help; we are here to support you.

Galatians 6:2 - "Carry each other's burdens, and in this way, you will fulfill the law of God."

Just keep trying, and you will achieve great things.

J

Philippians 3:14 - "I press on toward the goal to win the prize for which God has called me in Christ Jesus."

Kindness and determination are your superpowers.

Ephesians 4:32 - "Be kind and compassionate to one another, forgiving each other, just as God forgiven you."

Learning is a journey, and you're on the right path.

Proverbs 2:6 - "For the Lord gives wisdom; from his mouth come knowledge and understanding."

Mistakes are part of the learning process; embrace them.

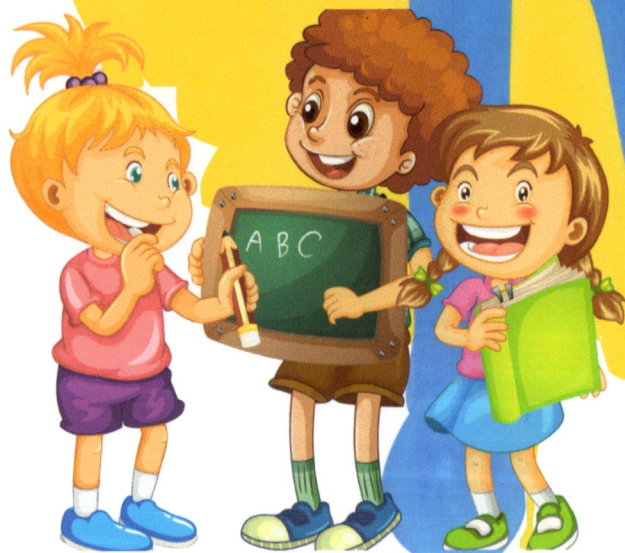

Proverbs 24:16 - "For though the righteous fall seven times, they rise again."

Never give up, you have the courage to overcome challenges.

Joshua 1:9 -"Be strong and courageous. Do not be afraid; do not be discouraged, for the Lord your God will be with you wherever you go."

Opportunities are endless for you, so dream big.

Jeremiah 29:11 - "For I know the plans I have for you, declares the Lord, plans to prosper and not for evil, to give you a future and a hope."

Perseverance leads to success; you've got it in you.

James 1:12 - "Blessed is the one who endures under testing and temptation, that person will receive the crown of life."

Questions are how we learn, keep asking and exploring.

Proverbs 2:3 - "Cry out for insight, and ask for understanding."

Remember, you are loved, just as you are.

1 John 4:16 - "So we have come to know and to believe the love that God has for us. God is love, and anyone who abides in love abides in God, and God abides in them."

Strength comes from within, and you have it abundantly.

Philippians 4:13 - "I can do all things through him who gives me strength."

Try your best, and that's always enough.

Galatians 6:9 - "Do not get tired of doing good, for you will be rewarded if you do not give up."

Understand that you're unique and that's a wonderful thing.

Jeremiah 1:5 - "Before I formed you in the womb I knew you, before you were born I set you apart."

Victory is in your future; keep moving forward.

1 Corinthians 15:57 - "But thanks be to God, who gives us the victory through our Lord Jesus Christ."

We're proud of your hard work and determination.

Isaiah 41:10 - "So do not fear, for I am with you; do not be dismayed, for I am your God. I will strengthen you and help you; I will uphold you with my righteous right hand."

Xerox copies are dull; you're an original masterpiece.

Ephesians 2:10 - "For we are God's handiwork, created in Christ Jesus to do good works, which God prepared in advance for us to do."

You are more than your challenges; you're a star.

Daniel 12:3 - "Those who are wise will shine like the brightness of the heavens, and those who lead many to righteousness, like the stars for ever and ever."

Zealous and determined, that's who you are!

Romans 12:11 - "Be enthusiastic and work hard for the Lord."

About the Author

Erika McCallister is a native of Louisiana and mom of 3 talented girls. She is a global engineer with a passion for STEM and Dyslexia awareness. As an avid reader throughout her life, she encouraged her girls to read and learn new things through lived experiences. After discovering that her brilliant twins learned differently than their peers, she fostered a new environment of learning while advocating for dyslexia awareness in schools and communities across the world. Erika currently lives in Texas where she supports her daughters with Double Trouble Press, a literary publishing company for those who are touched by kids with super powers. In this new adventure, she has taken the role of publishing director, author, editor, and illustrator. She walks through life believing her motto, "I'm sipping from my saucer, because my cup runneth over."

www.DoubleTrouble.Press

"Mom of two Authors who couldn't READ!"

www.ingramcontent.com/pod-product-compliance
Lightning Source LLC
Chambersburg PA
CBHW041428090426

42741CB00002B/77